How to Build a Stable Android Device Manager for Android TV Boxes

Build an Android Manager for Android TV Boxes - FREE!

I0424662

Copyright© 2019

By Mason Bolton III

Contents

Part One – The Introduction

What This Restore System Will Do For You

Congratulations on your decision to build an Android Management System for android TV systems!

Android TV boxes come out of the box practically brain dead.

The usual offerings will include a selection of video viewers, a web browser, and a bevy of tools to cast streams and manage your android system. I mean, really. These tools, however vital, barely scratch the surface of what your android box is capable to do.

Android TV boxes can send your TV viewing choices through the roof. However, they can do SO much more. Using your android TV box to its fullest potential will permit you to use your video center to check email, connect to social services, watch streams direct from internet, track your finances, and play games and so much more – all spontaneously from your easy chair.

Your Android TV box is a computer. Not a *dedicated* computer that is mostly a one-trick pony, but an *actual* computer, that can perform any computer task, such as tracking your calendar, surfing the web, reading PDF files, flying a flight simulator.

However, in practice, it is hardly possible to attain this level of performance without crashing your android box because the android TV box is shaky when operating in the android phone environment. That is why your "*out of the box*" offerings are so meager. You need to explore to determine the best configuration for your system.

This guide frees you from hours of rebuilding your system after a crash, and sets you on a course for true mastery for your android TV system.

That might not sound like much, but it means that you can **expand the use of your android TV box** into the *stratosphere*, and when (not if) it crashes, you will be ready to deal the matter *without rising from your comfort chair.*

This guide describes an Android Management system (AMS) to control the stability of your android TV box. It has been **tested** on systems as new as android nine and as archaic as android 4.5 (lollipop). These instructions perform equally on every system.

The alternative to an AMS recovery system is a **single application** that, once installed, takes over the process and ensures that your system is always stable and reliable. Now, what application would that be?

An AMS is the only method to reliably manage and control your android TV box. There simply exists no "one-stop" method to get it done.

To do this job effectively, you need a *system*. The system in your hands right now, will take the average recovery time for a severe crash from many hours (maybe **days**), down to about five minutes!

This tool is all about YOU. This is NOT a magic bullet. It is a **tool**, nothing more. Fueled by your imagination, this system is able to deal with a myriad of problems that plague android TV

Deploy this system, and you will use your android box for *everything*. You will check your email, observe your calendar, read PDF files, write a letter, play video streams, surf the net, play video directly from the internet – and much more – all from you easy chair!

This is precisely what you want an android box for. Additionally, this system will certainly transfer to ALL of your android TV boxes, so a little work will take you a LONG way.

What this book is NOT

This book is NOT an operator's manual for your android box, or *any* android box in particular. We will not delve into the mysteries of Alice or any particular tool or accessory.

This book seeks to acquaint you with the android box **beneath** the pretty face. We intend to suggest a method to build a secure system for running to explore your android TV box. We also seek to offer a fast method of recovery after crash so that you **expand** and **explore** your android TV box without fear.

This book is NOT a "go-to" resource for all things android. You won't get a round android education from reading this manual but you **will** learn more than you could from watching a video.

This book is NOT an attempt to please *everybody*. We **hope** you like it and find some of the ideas applicable to stabilizing your android TV box. If you have questions, we hope you will ask.

Who Can Build This Restore System?

YOU can build this system, no matter whom you are, no matter how technical non-proficient, no matter how bad you are at math.

Indeed, there is ZERO reason why; with the application of just a bit of work – and the ability to follow these SIMPLE instructions – YOU cannot have this system set up in about an hour.

We know that "tech stuff" can be scary.

Be assured though that there is no reason to be frightened of your android TV box.

It is certainly **not** going to be as stable as the computer sitting on your desktop at home. This is just one of those things that you will have to accept.

However, it is a mistake to sell your android TV box short. All of that power, just going to waste. What a shame.

Are you ready to make PROPER use of this marvelous tool?

Good. Let's get started.

The Advantages of Your Restore System

Android TV box really is a video revolution – or at least it will be – once it has grown up as a technology.

Android technology already performs satisfactorily in android telephones, but when it comes to TV boxes, not so much.

Android box operation is *complex*. You may see no need for these techniques during the honeymoon period (first year or so) but once the fun starts, it likely will not let up.

With a *proper* system in place, recovering your box is **not** difficult. It was never meant to be. The ***promise*** of the android TV box is just too seductive to ignore.

The android TV box permits you to attach a **full working computer** to your TV set, *any* TV set – just in case you were wondering. It does so in a *snap*.

Some "smart" TV sets already come with a suite of TV applications, all driven by *proprietary* operating systems. This means that most likely, Samsung™ and Vizio™ will use *different* systems to support your TV applications.

Android TV boxes go these systems one better. They install a **common** operating system to your TV set to give it *open source access* to online android programs. You also have an **unrestrained** access to the *complete* suite of applications that are just waiting for you over at the Google Play Store.

It is perhaps an over-simplification, but plainly put, Android TV boxes offer your television set ALL of the same capabilities as your *android phone*. It does so for *any television* on the market.

The Android Problem

Now, think about that for a moment, because as wonderful as it may sound, nevertheless, there is a problem. Android TV systems are inherently *unstable* in the android TV environment.

This is not the fault of the android operating system itself. Our problem actually has more to do with how the engineers put your android box together.

All of this may sound disappointing at first, but as usual, the solution is right in front of us. We simply need to *adjust our expectations*. That is...

If your android box is going to crash, then let us build a system to **stabilize** the android TV platform for *our* purposes.

The Mission Statement

Our purposes are to ensure that we gain ALL of the functionality that we want from our android TV boxes (not just "out of the box" offerings, and to ensure that we are back up and running again *fast* after crash. An Android Management System for *system stabilization* is the *perfect* solution.

The Mission Goals

Accomplishing our mission statement means achieving certain goals that are used to measure how well we have hit our mark. The goals in support of our mission statement are below.

Using AMS you will **attain** these goals – and **so** much more. A more complete listing of the benefits for your AMS restore system includes the following...

➤ To expand functionality of your android TV system (KEY benefit)
➤ To keep your android TV system clean and optimized
➤ To stabilize the android TV platform for your custom purposes
➤ To repair damaged and/or corrupted android TV box installations
➤ To ensure that you are back up FAST after a crash
➤ To obtain a faster and more efficient Network access
➤ To obtain "super" improved stability (compared to normal)
➤ To arrange for MANY fewer system crashes
➤ To provide for faster/smoother reboots/resets
➤ and more...

The *natural* vision of the android TV box is to provide all of the above without any special treatment. In theory, this is how the perfect android box would behave.

However, there are inherent weaknesses in the android TV box platform that act to defeat these natural benefits.

By way of compensation, though, please know that EACH of these weaknesses, YOU can identify, and even treat using he AMS.

It's a simple fact of android life.

If we want to raise our android box to its fullest measure of potential, then there is the serious and omnipresent risk of crashing your android TV box, and even fatally **destroying** it.

Part Two – The Discussion

The APK Files

We call the file that describes **how** to install (un-install) an application on your android box, an "APK" file. As such, the APK file has an extension of ".apk." Because your restore kit will help you to manage these files *specifically*, you need to understand what they are.

Talkin' APK

When you download an application from the Google™ Play Store to your android system that application does NOT install to your android system – whether TV box or phone.

Instead, the "Play Store" installs an "APK" file to your android TV box. Then it *executes* this file locally on your android box, and the *APK* then installs the application that you downloaded.

This process is ***important*** to understand, because this means that once we have installed the application, your android system *will not need the APK any longer*. The application is now resident on the android box, and the *application* is the only reason that we needed the APK file in the first place.

From the foregoing, it should be clear that an efficient way to conserve memory - of which your android TV box is **always** drastically short, is to *remove these APK files*.

Unfortunately, life is rarely so cooperative. For purposes of our restore system, we DO still have urgent need of these APK files.

Managed properly, these are the **life's blood** of your restore system. We cannot simply "throw them away." We have much work for them to do.

However, they cannot do the job alone. They work in conjunction with other tools named in this guide, and along with your own natural ability to solve simple problems.

About the Android Applications

You are free to download and try any applications that you like from Google™ Play Store. There are applications to stimulate your creativity and ignite your fantasies.

However, there is the *stability* problem to consider. For this reason, I *strongly* recommend using the suite of applications that you will find in this restore kit – at least to start.

We tested these applications for good stability in the repair system environment. In addition, they run the gamut for "needs" that you might want your restore kit to address. You will find file managers, extraction tools, PDF readers, video players and much more!

The Google™ Play Store Caveat

(For android TV box owners, logging onto Google™ Play Store can be dangerous. It will force update *to critical files that can be volatile to your android TV box. Remember that these updates likely think that they are updating android* **phones**.

You **will** *need to log onto Google™ Play Store to download needed APK files. There are* **better** *places on the internet to get these files, but we will not recommend them here, as they may be potentially illegal.*

If you use the play store, however, after you are done, you **must** *LOG OFF the Google™ Play Store, and test your box for issues. The best option is to* **reset** *your android box to remove any updates installed by the store.*

Perhaps the best way to approach this task, is to make a list and get EVERYTHING you need while logged on. Download these apps to a location on your android box (the Download folder will do) and move them using your file manager to a flash disk, or SD drive. Then, **reset** *(not reboot) your android box to remove possible updates.*

Do NOT reset your android box if you log in to the play store for only a few minutes for a quick update or something. In this case, reset is rarely necessary, since updates take a bit of time to commence. If you are SURE that no updates to your system occurred (you will know), then there is no need to reset your android TV box.

This next stop along our tour introduces us to the *"built-in"* applications. These applications are automatically installed (at reset only) as a part of your android system build.

You DO have some control over these applications, but you are NOT able to delete them. Fortunately, built-in applications are rarely volatile, and it is NEVER advisable to remove them.

Built-in applications NEVER install on reboot. They will only fresh install as the result of a **reset**.

As luck would have it, your AMS restore system sees these applications as simply a part of the environment. As such, they need no special handling.

Built-in applications include your web browser, a file browser (or file manager), a video player or two, applications to cast your video to remote devices and a host of other tools.

Some of these built-in applications are *system tools*, critical to the proper operation of your android TV box. Obviously, you want to leave these files alone, giving them a wide berth.

Itiis important to remember though that you can *recognize* the "built-in" applications - as opposed to the "pre-installed" applications, by testing to see of you can *delete* them.

To test, visit the *"Settings"* area of your system menus (each system will differ) and select *"Apps"* from the resulting menu.

Select the application in question and look carefully at the information now on screen.

There will be an item to "uninstall" your application. If no such choice occurs, or if it offers only the option to "disable" the application, then it is a built-in application and you need take no further action with it.

The Pre-Installed Applications:

Like built-in applications, the pre-installed applications install AUTOMATICALLY whenever you reset your android system.

It is worth repeating that this does NOT include power-on (after power-down), or normal boot up operations. Your system only needs to do this when you *reload* the android operating system, either by soft reset or by using the hard reset button.

Pre-installed applications are an offering for convenience, on the part of your android box manufacturer as a way quickly to set up your android TV box when disaster strikes. That's *exactly* what **this** AMS does. Make recovery easier should disaster strike.

Pre-installed offerings aren't usually too impressive. Mostly these will consist of tools to cast images to your phone, and the critical tools like a file viewer (not manager) and a browser that you likely will have to replace. Finally, there *might be* a (useless) movie utility or two that you **no doubt** will have to replace.

Actually, because of the volatile nature of these applications, the offerings are necessarily thin. To go safely beyond these offerings you need *protection* – which is what this book is all about.

When working with an android TV box, we must always be cognizant that - because there is no such thing as an android TV box application, the application *probably* thinks that your TV box is an android *phone*.

Fortunately, our system beats the odds again – as we enjoy the luxury to *ignore these applications also*. We do NOT have to remove them. Once again, though, there is a caveat.

Unlike built-in applications, pre-installed applications **are volatile**.

Consequently, it is best if we *remove* them from the system. This advice applies even if you never plan to **run** the application. Any application installed to your android system demands resources just to be there. If they install to your system, then they **affect** it – even if they are not actively running.

Moreover, many of these applications *keep running in the background,* to provide you with status reports, communications messages, application warnings etc.

These applications may conflict with your android system, *or they may conflict with each other.* Where your android system is concerned, "cleanliness really IS the next best thing to godliness."

Your Installed Applications:

This section describes your *installed* applications - the land of enchantment.

You want *power*. This class of applications will do that for you. The installed applications enable you to build a custom system, all your own. Learn to order pizza in your very own environment and you may retire to your easy chair and never rise again!

The *installed applications* suite is the *"Alice in Wonderland"* area of your AMS restore kit. It will enable your android system to offer you just about every computer experience imaginable.

This power comes at the very high *stability*, at least when using an android TV box, as opposed to an android phone.

Installing a new application to your android TV box is the most *dangerous* game in town. The application is ripe to crash your android system **horribly**, since you have not yet had the opportunity to test it.

Ideally, you should not to add new applications to your android environment - period. The collections of stable of applications that accompany this restore kit are suitable for most any need.

However, upgrades to the android operating system (currently at 9.0) will eventually obsolete even these applications, so be prepared to *maintain* the AMS kit by seeking valid updates or replacements.

We HAD to warn you about installing new apps, but we know that installing apps is what computers are all about. Inevitably, you **will** encounter that seductive application that will force you to attempt the upgrade. You will install it.

The results could be *frightening*. Your TV box could conceivably fall dead, and *never* rise again. Even if you replace it, the ***new*** box may become useless, if you try to load that application again.

However, despite all of this potential mayhem, if you want to try something new – we say – **go ahead**! The mayhem is easy to manage using this AMS restore system.

With AMS installed, you may *fearlessly* trudge forward to try your new applications with confidence, knowing that – whatever happens - with this system, you will be back up in *minutes*.

Just please be sure to read this **entire guide through**, before attempting to install a new application to your android box.

How to work with installed applications

There are two requirements for working with installed applications.

1. You must master how the *application* works.
2. You must master how *YOU* work with the application.

Mastering how the installed application works

You will address the first problem by reading the application instructions, usually downloaded to your system along with the application itself. Read that documentation and you will learn all that you need to master how the application works.

If after running the application your android system begins coughing up blood, try to decide if the *system* is wounded, the *application* is wounded, or – and this one is tricky – if the application *wounds the system.*

This area is a bit tricky. Learning to work with the application as a part of your android TV box, really is required of anyone who hopes to gain control over their android TV box. It seems, however that the concept seems cloudy to most people.

Actually, the concept is simple. Mastering how you work with the application refers to working with the application, from the *android point of view.* In short, you need to learn to think as your android box thinks. You need to see the world as it does.

Then, if a problem arises with loading and using an application, you need not ask yourself if your android TV box is misbehaving; **it is**.

Instead, we want to understand *why* the system has issues with this application. Is it incompatible? Is it corrupted? Did your android box corrupt it? Should we update the app, or replace it? Do we actually have both (or either) options *available* to us, given the nature of the crash?

These are but a *tiny* sample of the types of questions that you should ask yourself, always from the android boxes point of view. You must look for clues from the environment, and then devise a plan, using the new powers granted you by AMS, to probe these clues and determine the problem.

Actually, it's a load of fun, and you feel in control like never before, especially if you own an older box and would prefer not to buy a new one. Besides – new boxes crash too – they are all different - and they get **worse** over time

AMS might be a **better** solution than going for something new, UNLESS you *really* **know** your android TV boxes. In that case, just getting a box with your preferred launcher and maybe more robust streaming performance *might* be worth the trade.

We will talk more on troubleshooting specific issues that this restore system is able to manage, or to repair. We will also look at a few debug examples to teach you how to **use** your restore system.

For now though, we've a bit of technical learning in front of us. It won't be too involved, we promise you —but without knowledge, this restore system is worse than useless.

So — let's get to it...

Part Three – The Tech Stuff

Memory

To understand how to use AMS to its fullest, we really do need to understand the role of *memory* – and how your android TV box makes use of it.

Not to worry. Our treatment of memory will be *extremely* superficial. However, the concept of **memory corruption** will be the underlying cause of MANY of your problems – so you need to understand how your android system *uses* memory in order that we might understand how to manage these problems as they arise.

Memory Corrupts – Absolutely…

Android files reside in *memory* on the android system, and *running* android applications reside in applications memory.

Memory is a pool of electronic circuitry designed to hold electronic information. Your android application is an *example* of such data.

When you run an application from your android system, the program is put into *applications* memory so that the android box knows where it is, and has an immediate access to it.

If applications are *stored* to the android box memory, and if an application, *itself* might be corrupt, then a corrupted application can *corrupt the memory in your android box.*

That done; it is now entirely possible for your android box memory to infect a *clean* application! Think of it as a computer virus.

This is dangerous.

In a "normal" computer, the application is isolated from the *"actual" operating* system by running all applications in a protected *copy* of the operating system. The actual operating system remains safely stored away on your disk drive. Then, if the computer crashes *as the result of an application*, it will ALWAYS be possible to restore it.

This is similarly true of your android telephone. While it may possess no hard drive, the system protects the operating system in the same way as described above.

The information simply is stored on an electronic device instead of a hard drive. In both these systems, stability is nearly infallible, because this isolation *protects* the operating system.

NO SO, with the Android TV Box. This fact marks the BIGGEST difference between your android TV box and regular computer systems – or even android telephones. Within the android TV box, there *exist **no** separation services*. Thus, ALL memory can corrupt from *any* source, even by a running application! Your android box is wide open. No *wonder* it crashes!

Worse, if everything on your android box is subject to *be* corrupted – **then** that means EVERYTHING on your TV box is *subject* to **CAUSE** corruption.

There are times that an application will crash your android TV system so hard that it will not even reset! That is why you have a "hard reset" switch on EVERY android system.

The maker of your android box **understands** that your android TV box (*any* android TV box, at any price) eventually will fail beyond your ability to **restore** it. Without this hard reset function, your box would lock you out of your android TV system *forever* – with absolutely **no** way back into it.

While this is a *true* vulnerability of your android TV box, it is **not** a problem, per se. This is an *expected* design function. It is a sane and reasonable compromise. Can you imagine how the cost of one of these boxes would *skyrocket* if the manufacturers attempted to make it as bullet proof as your desktop computer system?

Pick up your android box and hold it in your hand. Note that it weighs only about half a pound. Now, go and lift the computer system sitting on your desktop. Big difference? You bet!

The moral of the story is this: *it is perfectly natural for your android system to crash* – often. It is a computer system designed for one basic (*volatile*) operation (*streaming is* **volatile**) and its manufacturers plan to sell it cheap. You android box is **not** broken. Stop clobbering it. It is what it is. There is **nothing** for you to fix.

Why do Android TV Systems Crash?

There are in fact *many* reasons why your android TV box crashes so often.

We have already looked at memory corruption, though we still need to understand how to determine just **what** in the system has corrupted, or where that happened.

We have discussed the fact that most of these applications actually expect to be running on an android phone. Indeed, the majority of apps that you will use certainly DO assume that they ARE running on an android phone. This is an obvious point of incompatibility.

Clearly, an application *friendly* to an android phone stands a better than fair chance to be *unfriendly* to your android TV system. Despite the fact that both run the android operating system, these are *completely different* devices.

Therefore, the **most direct solution** to obtaining a stable performance is to use only applications that are compatible with your android TV system – and NOT your android phone.

However… just **which** applications would those be? As we noted earlier, whoever heard of an android TV application? The android application stores can't help. They offer applications only designed to be truly compatible with android *phones*.

We will not name the specific guilty applications here, since they might clean up to work properly with your box at any time. They may also be compatible with one android system, and not another.

However, any applications that we mention here were chose with care. We selected them for function, and tested them for compatibility with **all** the other applications. This ensures stability for your android TV platform, no matter what application is running.

Selecting an Application Diet

In android TV, as with all computer applications, you must pay strict attention as to WHAT applications you run, on your system.

You will benefit much by thinking about HOW you use your android TV box. Naturally, it is best to have set this profile before you buy your android TV box, but, strictly speaking, this is not possible. Android boxes differ **wildly** amongst different manufacturers. About the only way to determine the viability of an application for your android box is to *test* it.

This means of course, that your system might crash and never return. Obviously, without an AMS, it would be foolish even to *consider* such a risk.

On the other hand, you take such a risk as this any time that you run any application at all! For example, using your internet browser is just about the most dangerous thing you can do with your android box.

One obvious solution to this problem is NOT to use your internet browser. If you do this, you will remain stable for a very long time.

However, while stability is important, chucking your browser is a **terrible** price to pay. The solution is unacceptable.

Perhaps a better idea is to **use** your android TV system however you want, whenever you want - KNOWING that it will crash sooner than later, and then utilize the tools in this AMS restore kit to get back up and running – FAST.

If you have an android box on which you have given up, have a second look at it. The means to *tame* that system (AMS) is in in your hands, right now.

The Network

As anxious as you must be to get started, we STILL have preparations to make. We will take a moment here for a quick discussion of the **network**.

Be patient, please. Getting at the "Meat and Potatoes" is certainly, where the action is, but of course, we know that there is **value** to the Brussels sprouts as well.

A Friend Indeed...

On a desktop computer (and android phone), the "network" is *very much* your friend. Imagine how useless your desktop computer system, laptop or cell phone would be if it were permanently to disconnect from all networking functions. No online banking, no email for aunt Bess, no way to text that special someone.

On an android TV box, though, the network definitely is NOT your friend. Indeed, sadly, we must conclude networking of any kind to be your android box' **worst** enemy. Unchecked, it can crash your system within minutes, and even **destroy** your ability to use that box again – ever (if not for the hardware reset button).

We observed earlier that the only way to avoid this problem is NOT to use your android browser, but we *also* decided this too high a price to accept it as a solution. We want to USE that browser, *without* inflicting pain upon ourselves.

Fortunately, AMS rides to the rescue again. With this restore system installed to your android box; this near fantasy becomes an **easy** reality. Start with a **clean** network, and everything else just falls into place.

Naturally then, you always want to **test your network** every time that you start a session on your system. Equally important, *you want to use only the built-in browser application to do this.*

This rule is a *"prime directive,"* unless you have experimented with a browser application beforehand and determined it safe for use; you should use only the built-in browser for network communications.

If you like, you can visit the browser "settings" menu to set up location blocking, to select the browser type and to set other browser preferences.

What is a Network?

ALL home networks today operate similarly. They are low maintenance. They are wireless. They use an "access point" to scrub the airwaves looking for messages that mean to talk to one of its connected network neighbors.

For example, your android TV box sends messages to your access point to be sent to another device on your network, or perhaps out onto the internet. Naturally, any information coming from the internet in response to your message is addressed to **your access point** (via your network access provider).

The access point then finds your android box (in its database) and sends the message there.

The access point **sorts** the messages, so that neither your cell phone, desktop computer nor any other device connected to this access point will receive the message in error. Only the intended target actually sees the message.

Network Settings

Set only such browser preferences, as you must. *You don't want a hundred settings to wade through, every time that you restore your android box. You cannot **save** these settings, so you are advised to keep things simple.*

Your settings **will** survive most system *reboots (unlike system resets)*; but they **can** seemingly have a mind of their own - coming and going unpredictably.

If the settings are very few, consequently they are little trouble to set up again after system reset. Upon reset – **all system settings are lost.**

More Method than Madness

It may not be obvious, but the **method** that you use to bring up your network is rather critical for system stability.

Your access point can be set up by way of a Wired Equivalent Privacy (WEP) code that you type in (to endless exhaustion) or, alternatively, a Wi-Fi Protected System (WPS) where you simply press a "blue" button on the access point itself and – voila – you are connected.

BOTH methods are **fine**, however as you might imagine, pressing the blue button once, beats entering some sixty hexadecimal numbers into your android TV box every time your network needs rebooting. Holding to the general theory, the more that you use your android box, the more you will need to reboot it.

Take note though, that the convenience of the button – as seductive as it is – is NOT the sole reason to make this recommendation. Experience shows that using the blue "WPS" button seems to be the more *persistent* option, as well.

Bring your network up on this method, and it is mostly set and forget. Usually, it takes a reset (not a reboot) to bring down the network if installed via the blue button, whereas using the WEP code is fragile, at its best.

At this point, we have completed our discussion of what makes your android box fail, and are ready to take the next logical step.

That is – we will learn the *types* of failure that might occur.

The Types of Failure
The Corrupted Application

The corrupted application is easy to recognize. Yesterday it was working. Today, it is not.

The simplest way to handle a corrupted application is to attempt to update. To do this, simply re-install the application without first removing it. Often, this procedure will rewrite the critical resource files, restoring the application to its previous healthful state.

Naturally, you may attempt to rouse the application by rewriting forcing the application to acquire new **resource** information. To do this, you must clear the *program* cache (not the *system* cache) by selecting the application from the "Apps" menu. There you will see options to clear the application caches.

However, as you might have guessed, sometimes this procedure fails. Then, the proper course, as you might imagine is to remove the application and to re-install it in place. If the application was merely corrupted, this will restore it.

Should re-installation fail, then something is now different about your android installation from when you made a last successful installation. A reset is your best fix. Should reset fail ever, you must resign yourself to a **full** system wipe.

The Failure UPON Installation

Your android TV box will fail for a myriad variety of reasons.

Fortunately, testing a *failing application* is very straightforward. Most applications incompatible with your android box will fail on installation. Then, you have your answer.

Of course, there is the exception. The application will load, but upon invocation, it will cause numerous system errors. Most of these errors are invisible in normal operation.

These failures may not be fatal to your system – at least not immediately. The application may crash within a few hours (or days), but if you are able to make your use of it, you might opt to use the application in any case. Afterward, you would *reboot* your box and remove the application using the normal system tools.

This seems a good time to point out that, whenever you suspect that, a failing application has crashed your android box, you should **reboot**, as opposed to reset. You should reserve resets solely to *repair* serious **system** problems.

The Failure to Install

We have just seen a situation where a faulty application might **install** badly.

In this section, we will meet defective applications, which fail to install at all. The install procedure will *seem* to work, but the application will not actually *load* onto your android box.

Failure to install is not the most common occurrence, but it is not rare either. We mention it here in the context of this restore kit so that you understand your course of action if the issue should occur.

Failure to install can be immediately serious, or it may look completely benign. Your system may turn up its nose and refuse to take the application, or it may swallow the application with no evidence of trouble, until you attempt to find and use the application, and find that it is **not** there.

Your first move should be to *remove the application*. The application might have installed, even if you cannot see it. If it **uninstalls**, then you are good, and no reboot should be necessary. You may simply attempt to install it again - IF you have the nerve.

If, however, the uninstall attempt **fails**, and the application does NOT show up on your system, then it probably actually did **not** install. You cannot *uninstall* what did NOT *install*. Therefore, the uninstall attempt **will** fail. ***Despite the failure, try to install the application again.*** If it appears, uninstall it – and do NOT attempt to install it again.

While it may be possible to uninstall and reinstall a failure to install, the best course of action is to use a default application from this restore kit to perform your task, and then **reboot** your android box. If, a few reboots fail – then reset is unavoidable.

*Please note that, when using this AMS restore kit, to **reset** your system will be nearly as simple as to reboot it, but a reset "deep cleans" your system and memory caches, reformats your android TV box and rebuilds all critical system files. Reset your box whenever it seems sluggish and error prone.*

The Failure to Reside

This type of application failure is a bit more insidious. The "Failure to Reside" means that your system properly installed an application, and you have been using it, until your system experiences a fatal crash. You will need to reboot the android box.

Upon rebooting your system, you notice that one or more of your android applications are missing. You can check your applications listing, but we can save you some time. You will NOT find these missing applications anywhere on your system (*bummer*).

Our immediate response is to **reset the system** using the software "reset" command from your system menus (see your guide) or the "hard reset" button, mentioned earlier.

Sometimes you can put the offending application(s) back in place without issue. If this works, and you don't want to lose the immediate system for some reason, you can just continue on working, until a **fatal** crash occurs.

You **can** afford this crash, whenever it might happen. To get you back up and operating again within a few minutes is the **goal** of this restore system. Perhaps now you begin to see how this AMS restore kit **frees** you to explore the full potential of your android box. This is only the beginning.

The Failure to Uninstall

We already met the application that will not install, and the application that installs badly. Now meet the neer-do-well cousin. This is a barnacle of a cuss that, refusing to make its own way in the world – moves into your android TV box, and just won't leave. You will try everything to shake it loose, but it refuses to let go.

Such an application is simply "stuck" in your android TV box. You cannot uninstall the application, cannot even see it on the system.

However, your box still may operate perfectly (for your purposes) and it may continue to do so for some time. The only issue here is if the "stuck" application is a critical one. For example, if you are reading a PDF and the PDF reader becomes "stuck" then you have *lost* the application.

Here's why...

You cannot *uninstall* an application, when it is stuck. It truly is in limbo, having ferreted out place to hide where you simply cannot get to it.

You cannot *delete* or *update* a "stuck" application, because the system says it did not install to begin with. You cannot *install* the application because the android box' corrupted guts tell it that it actually **is** on board – and must *uninstall* first.

Thus, you cannot uninstall the PDF reader, nor can you install it again – so the application is **lost**. You cannot use this application again until after a reset of your android box.

HOWEVER, You CAN install a *different* PDF reader for *temporary* use from the AMS safe stores – to get you through until a better time – when the opportunity for "reset" can present itself.

Of course, if you have "stuck" applications that you cannot remove, then your android box is NOT performing properly. The proper course is to **reset** the system – but **you** have an alternative.

With this, AMS restore system you are now above *consequences*, and can do whatever you want. If you go on using your android TV box in the meantime – what is it going to do - **crash**? This guide and the restore system that it describes, perfectly prepare us for this eventuality.

Therefore, in this situation, the best remedy is to ***use your system until it crashes***. *Then* reset (in this instance) the TV box.

Part Four – The Construction

How to Reset and Reboot Your Android TV Box
To Reboot or to Reset: THAT is the Question...

Frankly, the skill to know *when* to reboot your android TV box is mostly a fine art. The only comfort we can offer is to point out that, by understanding how your system works, you **will** be able to determine **by the symptoms**, what procedure best to deploy in a particular situation.

Note that debugging these issues using AMS is not difficult. Actually, the process is quite easy. Indeed, with this system in hand, it is both possible and practical simply to reset your box at the first sign of trouble – but *please refrain from doing this*.

This really is NOT the proper way to do things. You will learn later that using AMS; it pays to give some thought to just WHY your system is crashing. After all, you are after stability, not a new and fancy rebooting method.

To this end, you need to include *yourself* in the equation. You have both instincts and brains. Your AMS restore system (desperately lacking both) plainly NEEDS these resources (from **you**). Please do not hesitate to offer them.

The "RESET" Types

There really are only two types of reset.

1. The Hard reset
2. The Soft reset

The Hard reset

Most times, you will use a *reboot* to restore your android system. There are times, though, that your box will crash hard and not respond to a reboot request.

When this happens, you will **reset** your android box.

Occasionally though, even a reset will not rouse your system. It just dies at the boot logo.

A **hard reset** makes use of the reset port on the side or bottom of your android TV box. A small switch resides inside this hole, and if you depress this switch and power up your unit, holding the switch in as you do so – the box will reset itself in about twenty seconds. From there, you may follow the simple instructions that are printed on screen to restore your android system.

Tip: *Keep a small straw (ballpoint pen ink filler tubes work great) permanently mounted in this hole, so when your android system requires reset, the entire restore system is ready to go.*

The Soft reset

The "soft reset" is very effective. It will clean your system well beyond what a simple reboot is capable.

However, it is not 100% reliable and it is possible that it will not clean your system completely.

In addition, the soft reset menus can activate only from your android desktop. If you cannot reach your desktop, then the process is not accessible.

You will not need the "AC clicker" to perform a soft reset. Just select a soft reset from the "Applications/"Backup & Reset" menu.

The system will reformat and restore itself to a default "clean" state. However, this process (as well as hard reset) takes **all** of system settings with it.

This is why we caution you NEVER to log on to any application. There is no social site that you cannot log onto direct over the internet and save your password logon there.

This is **more** than a friendly suggestion. Upon reset, you will need to remake ALL of your logins to all applications to restore your system to completion.

However, an application can corrupt, repeatedly, keeping you jumping through hoops, until finally you realize that the application *itself* is crashing your computer.

Your online logons might be lost to the browser, but remain intact and will easily restore by just logging on. These passwords are then bulletproof so long as the network works properly.

If you want to reach Twitter (for example), use your **browser** to contact your account. Your browser can also reach your Google email and calendar accounts and other online resources. That's what it's for!

To make best use of this restore system, you should begin thinking about how you might do things *differently*, so that resets of your system are as few and as painless as is possible.

Getting Set Up

For our purposes, we need to understand only a few vital things to develop our debug strategy. A trouble-shooting chart or anything of the kind is pure overkill. Below, we will describe the most important considerations for you to know. These will serve you just fine.

Remember that even if you decide to reset your box (the very harshest remedy) you will be back up and running again in five minutes, or so. Strictly speaking then, *reset* is always an alternative.

How well you manage your android TV box has everything to do with its stability. The real trick is to know just what you should do.

This guide will offer much help in that regard, but as the operator, you need to keep several things in mind whenever you tackle an issue with your android TV box.

These are the "prime directives" that should always be borne in mind when working with your TV box. If you need to, please record these steps to an index card and keep it with your android box. You **will** need them.

When managing your android box, *remember* these *key points*:

1. You must **ALWAYS** CHECK YOUR NETWORK WHENEVER YOU REBOOT/RESET your android TV box, even after a simple power-down.

2. Be **quick** to reset your android TV box, any time you determine that your **network** application does not function properly.

3. Reboot your box **several times**, until you get a stable boot.

4. Reset your TV box only *once*. A second reset is rarely necessary.

   MOST of the time a reboot will restore your system. However, it is a mistake to expect (or even to trust) a single boot of your computer. Your system may look grand, may perform like a demon, but will crash horribly first chance it gets.

Your best bet to get a good boot is to **watch the network**. The network leads the way.

If your network comes up fast, clean and unobstructed, you are likely on a good system, and might just as well use it until it crashes again. At all times, whether you reboot or reset is strictly up to you. Actually, with this restore system in place, the difference is hardly worth mentioning, since you will be back up in minutes, either way.

However, **without** AMS, a reset of your android box (*which MUST be done eventually*), will cost you hours, and could cost you *days*, to restore your system to where you were when your android box went down.

Now, you **think** *about that…*

Meet the Tools

In this chapter, we describe the tools you need to construct fully your android TV Active Management System.

First stop we have a look at the "hardware" tools set. Then we will move to undertake a discussion of the "software" tools.

How to Construct Your Android TV Box Restore Kit
The Preparation

In this chapter, we will commence actually to **build** our AMS: Android TV System Restore Kit.

You will need to be sure that you have obtained ALL of the items recommended earlier. You should also have your android box in house, powered up to a functional desktop (first boot after reset).

Test your network. Since we are in first boot after reset, the network will be fine. Nevertheless, **test it anyway**. It is good to develop the habit.

You should understand what we mean by the term "APK" and you should understand why it is important to installing and uninstalling your applications.

Finally, you should have READ and UNDERSTOOD every foregoing page of this manual. If you "cheated" by "jumping" to this chapter, you will be ill prepared to USE your restore system – even should you manage to construct it. *Read the manual.* Play by the rules, and you can expect jaw-dropping results.

The Hardware Tools:

Your complete AMS system will require a few tidbits of additional equipment that you may have already just lying around. None of this stuff is expensive, but you **do need** everything listed below. If you do not have this equipment, please collect it forthwith from your local hardware store.

- A **remote** AC outlet control

Controls AC power, so you can reboot /reset from your easy chair.

- A 500MB (or **greater**) SD card (best) or USB flash drive:

Supports a clean system store.

- An electrical extension outlet (with eight outlets).

Where we will "plug up" the remote AC outlet switch

Choose your SD card with care. You won't need much space to hold the "safe" applications stores, but SD memory expands your storage to many gigabytes if you wish.

These cards are comparatively cheap – so why not take advantage of a large one. Your android box will thank your with a faster and smoother performance.

The Software Tools:

The "software tools" will all be available on your android system. Either they are there already, or you will **put** them there under the direction of this guide.

These items will cost you nothing, save the time required to download and install these *free* applications.

The software tools are actually more important than the hardware tools. These are actually a list of screened and tested applications that perform the job of actually *rebuilding* your android system after crash, and maintaining best stability **after** your system restores.

APK Cleanup Image {Folder}; APK Files:

- CloudTV CTV-B-20141003.apk
- Faceguide 3.7.apk
- Kodi 16.1.apk
- MX Player 1.7.24.apk
- Netflix 2.4.1 build 950.apk
- Show Box 4.65.apk
- TeaTV 8.5r.apk
- Twitter 4.1.8.apk

Latest APK Image {Folder}; APK Files:

- Adobe Acrobat 18.2.0.182935.apk
- Advanced Task Manager 6.4.0.apk
- Alarm-clock-2-7-1.apk
- APK Export 3.2.4.apk
- File Manager 1.12.17.apk
- Finance 3.2.2.apk
- Ghostery-privacy-browser-2-0-7.apk
- Jota-text-editor-0-2-35-multi-android.apk
- LastPass Password Manager Premium 4.4.1842.apk
- Pdf-reader-3-2-4.apk

- Pdf-reader-5-9.apk
- Rotation Control 1.0.apk*
- VLC 3.0.11.apk*
- WiFi Automatic 1.7.8.apk
- WiFiReEnabler 1.10.20130722.apk
- YouTube 13.24.59.apk*

DO NOT install these files now. They are not safe as they are. The must be *properly* installed to your AMS restore system - and properly *used*, as well, to do the job they are intended to do.

The above is **not** a list of recommendations by any means. NO money exchanged hands to list these applications here. They simply exhibit characteristics beneficial to the restore mission of this guide.

Building the AMS Android Management System

In this section, we will introduce the "blueprint" for putting your restore kit together.

You will not learn how to *use* the restore system just yet. You need first to *build* your restore environment, and, in any case, trying to tackle this now would take us too far afield of the main course.

Below is the list of steps that you will need to take in order to build your restore kit. Use this list to "map" your position in the overall process as you go forward. Please study this list **before** getting started, as the familiarity will be your best friend when you begin the actual construction.

The "A" List

1. *Clean your system* -- Start your build with a clean reset.

2. *Download a file manager* -- You need a file manager to build your directories.

3. *Build the two directories as given above* -- These are the "APK Cleanup Image" and "Latest APK Image," directories. You should create these directories **directly** to your SD card or USB drive.

4. *Collect the APK files that will constitute your restore kit.*

5. *Extract APK files for pre-installed applications.*

6. *COPY the APK files from your android TV box to the directories on your SD card* (preferred) or USB flash drive (permanently mounted). This is a bit tricky. We will look at how to do this.

7. *Delete any APK files remaining on your android system.*

8. *BACKUP your directories* -- in case the copies on your SD card become corrupted.

9. *Set up your remote AC clicker* -- You will use this switch to remote reboot the android box. Plug the switch into your AC outlet and the android box into the remote controlled outlet ON the switch.

10. *REMOVE the File Manager and Extractor* – You will not need these, anymore. Keep these files as APK files in "safe" stores. In future, use the **default** file *browser* to move and edit files.

11. *REBOOT your android TV Box*

Once more – with feeling...

In this section, we take each step from the list above and flesh out each item. As you read, try to derive the *psychology* behind each step. The more you understand these steps as *one system*, the more benefit they will be to you.

With that, let us get started...

Clean your system

Power your box down, and use the **hard reset** procedure to reset it. This is the cleanest possible state that you can attain.

You can use a short straw to permanently occupy the reset portal (ballpoint pen filler tubes work great), so that when you need a hard reset, you need not search for a tool (difficult to find) to press the reset button. It is already, and forever right there.

Download a File Manager

This step *might* be optional. Many default installations for android TV boxes include a file *browser,* for **basic file operations**. With this file browser, you can see files, copy them, even move them, *but you cannot create directories* – which you desperately need to develop your restore system.

If your file browser is thus limited, you will need to install a file *manager*, which can attach you to the cloud, make directories, and perform a host of other advanced file functions. There is, in fact, such an application built into your restore kit.

In testing, most file browsers were volatile (for TV boxes), eventually causing a system crash. That is why it is so important that you stick to the "safe" files in the safe application stores.

Indeed, **most** functionality that you will need (including a file manager) will be available to you in the restore kit stores. You no longer need to worry about how to get **stable** copies of your favorite applications. They will be there for you, any time that you need them.

Collect your APK files

Obviously, you will first need to collect the APK files for the items that you want to store in your databases. These restore kit "stores" form the infrastructure for your restore kit.

You will (automatically) obtain an APK file for any application that you collect from the Google™ Play Store or other online sources. These APK files can simply move into the *safe resource stores*.

Please note, however, that any application file installed by *default* (after a reset) will need to be **_extracted_** to obtain the APK file to re-install this application. You may also need to "extract" any applications whose APK files are lost, or that have become corrupted. After extraction, these files also will move to the *safe resource stores* so you can re-install them easily if needed.

Build the two directories as given above

Use your File Manager, to build TWO directories **directly** onto your flash drive or your SD card.

There is no trick to using a file manager to create two directories on your SD card or on your USB flash drive. Both of these locations will appear in your file manager (or browser) as external media.

These directories are important, although it is probably premature to discuss our *need* for these at present. First, we must understand how to manage the *contents* of these directories.

If you find yourself confused when proceeding through these steps, you may return to the summary list of steps to map out where you are in the overall process.

APK Cleanup Image {Directory}

The "APK Cleanup Image" directory is a database of all files that your android box installs automatically to your system after reset (not reboot).

In the main, you must remove ALL of these applications from your android TV box. These applications are usually VERY volatile. In addition, with the *safe resource stores* at your disposal, you really won't need these additional applications.

The "Latest APK Image." database consists of all files that *YOU install by choice* to your android TV box. *Theoretically*, these can be any file in the play store, which is compatible with your TV box.

Some of these files can be of immense value to you, while others are quite volatile, so you need to tread carefully. As a general rule of thumb: simple applications are more stable than complex applications.

That said, the Google™ Play Store is chock FULL of many slick and even exciting applications, running the gamut from mystery games (for you detective types out there) to backgammon to spreadsheets, to calendars to just about any application you can name.

Feel **free** to explore these offerings. That is precisely what this AMS system encourages you to do. **If** a crash occurs, rebooting your computer will be as easy as can be – and you will never even leave your easy chair.

The APK files in this directory database are all available for installation, but AMS requires that **you do not install these applications until needed.**

This feature of AMS intends to increase the stability of your android box, while enabling you access to a **clean** version of your application(s) for easy installation *at any time*.

Forty applications are demanding resources and computing cycles from your ever-stressed android TV box certainly will crash it. You don't **need** those forty applications **today**. Select the applications that you use daily, and install the others only as you need them.

Your android box will be more stable, more reliable and more useful in its everyday service to your life.

Below are the **default** AMS restore kit stores. Feel free to add your own applications (after testing) for your use.

- Adobe Acrobat 18.2.0.182935.apk

Yep, our old friend. Permits reading and working with APK files.

- Advanced Task Manager 6.4.0.apk

A fun program to kill tasks, free up memory, save battery life, and more...

- Alarm-clock-2-7-1.apk

Everybody needs an alarm clock. Set this one from your easy chair

- APK Export 3.2.4.apk

Your APK extractor. Like a parachute, you will not need it often, but when you need it, you really need it.

- File Manager 1.12.17.apk

Goes beyond the file browser to enable directory creation, file management and more…

- Finance 3.2.2.apk

Yahoo finance. Keep up with your investments right from your easy chair.

- Ghostery-privacy-browser-2-0-7.apk

Next best thing to a VPN for keeping your surfing activities private.

- Jota-text-editor-0-2-35-multi-android.apk

A text editor is a vital tool for any fully capable computer system.

- LastPass Password Manager Premium 4.4.1842.apk

Use one logon to store ALL your passwords for easy login. It works well, but you STILL should not log onto your android system. Make any logons online.

- Pdf-reader-3-2-4.apk

This PDF reader has proven itself very stable.

- Pdf-reader-5-9.apk

Another GREAT application for reading PDF files.

- Rotation Control 1.0.apk*

Need to rotate your screen orientation for a particular application? Try this tool...

- VLC 3.0.11.apk*

A full-featured video streamer. Offered for completeness. You should use only default video streamers with your AMS restore kit.

- WiFi Automatic 1.7.8.apk

Might offer relief with some unstable networks.

- WiFiReEnabler 1.10.20130722.apk

Might help stabilize network dropping.

- YouTube 13.24.59.apk*

A critical tool, offered mostly for completeness. DO NOT USE. You should log onto your You Tube account ONLINE, via the default browser.

You should remember that **all** of these default applications are thoroughly *tested*. For any application that you see here, perhaps upwards of five others have been installed, tested and **rejected** for volatility, reliability or for other reasons.

These survivor applications should serve you well until you have an opportunity to download and test custom applications for yourself. Please DO take advantage of them.

Storing the Cleanup Files

You will remember from our earlier discussions that you must *extract* these files, if you are to obtain APK files for them. We haven't the choice to ignore these files. To build a complete restore environment, we must **make** these extractions and store the resulting APK file to the *safe resource file* environment.

Use the "Uninstall" procedure discussed previously to remove these default installed applications. Time does march on, and the installer in this kit might be obsolete due to operating system upgrades and the like. In that event, just snag a good installer/uninstaller off line that includes BOTH functions and include it in your AMS resource stores.

Recall that you must install ONLY those files to your system that you select *personally* for installation – **after** you test them. These default APK files do NOT meet that definition. These default APK files are *dangerous*.

Now, let us sample these automatically installed programs to get a flavor for what they are. Note that the applications given here were as taken from our test units. On your system these default applications may vary, but **whatever they are**, you *must* be prepared to *remove* them.

- CloudTV CTV-B-20141003.apk
- Faceguide 3.7.apk
- Kodi 16.1.apk

- MX Player 1.7.24.apk
- Netflix 2.4.1 build 950.apk
- Show Box 4.65.apk
- Twitter 4.1.8.apk

You will find these files listed innocuously among your other system applications such as your stream caster or default video player. The difference is that these are *user* applications. They are not tools. You do NOT critically need them. If you *really* want to install one of these applications, you deserve the right to test it first. Therefore, we must remove them. Let us do that now.

If you followed directions, your AMS restore system will list ALL of these applications to your installer, probably right in order at the top of your application listing. Wherever they appear, just mark and *remove* them with a click.

Extracting your files...

For our purposes, we will assume that you need to extract ALL of the application files previously listed. This will likely not be the case, but the exercise is more instructive than just salvaging one or two application files.

To begin, install the application from the restore kit stores; named "APK Export 3.2.4.apk" We will use this APK file to build your private "play store." If you do not have this file, download it now from the play store – as well as ALL of the other files in the restore kit stores list above.

When you are ready, we can proceed…

Using the extractor...

All of these applications are a snap to use, and the APK extractor is no exception. It does one job – extract your applications into an APK file – and it does this very well.

For your part, you need only select ("mark") the item and click on the "Save" button. This will move straight away to build clean APK files for every (marked) application **installed** to your android system. The APK files will be stored to your android TV box, where they are not safe, so we will move them directly.

Have you forgotten? *We do not want to store applications for any appreciable length of time on the android TV box.*

Most of these will be preinstalled applications that you can simply remove never to install again. But, if there may be applications that you **do** want to install, then extract them to your android TV box but do NOT install them.

Now, **extract** these files all at once as APK files. Copy these files immediately to minimize the potential for corruption. Then we will store these files to the AMS safe stores in case you need to reinstall them. No sense extracting them per each crash, is there?

Before we leave this discussion, please permit a final word on extraction.

Remember that for every moment an application file remains on your android system, another application – *or the android system itself* – threaten to corrupt it.

The obvious solution is to move your APK files from the android system to your SD card **as soon as possible.**

Getting Caught Up

With a complete suite of applications aboard, you would think us just about ready to "fly" our AMS restore system. Not so! We **still** have a few concepts to bring home.

The first challenge is met. We have seen how to insert/remove these APK applications to or from our android environment using the built-in application installer.

Our second encounter is with our old acquaintance, memory corruption. We have learned that applications *corrupt* android TV boxes and android TV boxes *corrupt* applications. If you are not careful, it will not be long before you are replacing your corrupted applications files with – you guessed it – *corrupted applications files!*

It is rather like using a friend's bath water. You will be taking YOUR dirt off – and putting HIS dirt on! Just as you need to start with clean bath water for good results, you need a source of clean *applications*. Otherwise, every time you reboot your system, you will be loading corrupted data to it.

We learned that when fighting corruption issues, replacing the failing applications may not help, for these might be corrupt, as well.

THAT is why you created the two directories. They will solve BOTH problems, by building two database archives that hold **clean** versions of our custom favorite applications for easy and safe installation to the environment.

Using the Application Un-installer

Since we are using the **built-in** application installer, you do not need to download any application to install or uninstall an APK application. You will find a suitable installer application right there, among your built-in applications, whenever you boot your system.

In case your version of android has a different installer on board, we will recommend loading the version found in the resource stores to install/uninstall the AMS kit files. This product supports a friendly interface that is in short supply across installers at large.

We will use this installer in deference to any other. You should use an alternative installer ONLY if the installer in the AMS stores will not function in your android version.

Using the installer could NOT be simpler. You just select (mark) an application(s) from the list, and then select **"Un-Install"** from the main menu (three vertical dots at top right corner of screen).

The application(s) will remove from your android TV box.

Using the Application installer

Installing items is equally easy. This is one of the main benefits of the restore system design. You manage the install and removal of applications (something you will do a LOT) from one central application.

As an example, consider the situation where you have just **uninstalled** *several* applications and you want to install **two** new applications. In this situation, the items you removed are still "marked." Our first duty is to clear them.

Just visit the menu again to find "Unselect All." This will clear **all** marked items.

Then, simply "mark" the items that you want to install. Remember to install only what you plan to use right now. Additional (clean) APK application will always be on your SD card (or USB flash) for later installation in a - well - *flash*.

Now select "Install" from the menu and your android system will install each application one by one. When it finishes its work, the items will be all in place – and ready for you to use.

Load Directories with APK Files.

Now that we have the applications extracted, it is time to load them to the two directories that we created earlier.

Bear in mind the *purpose* of these two directories as you load them. You want to get the proper results from the AMS when you use it to restore your system in practice.

In case that information has escaped you, let us reiterate.

Use the directory named "APK Cleanup Image" quickly to remove the *preinstalled* applications that are rather a **bear** to remove one by one. Set this directory up properly to remove ALL of these applications as efficiently as possible.

Use the directory named "Latest APK Image," quickly to **install** ALL of the files needed to *restore* your android system *fully,* with a single click.

You also want to use this directory for debug and repair of corruption issues, by reinstalling applications, or updating them.

The Directory Listing Order

The built in application installer on your android TV system probably has similar functionality to all the others on any android flavor that you care to name. The application installer supports a wonderful (and stable) installation environment that offers all the tools you need to enable your restore kit build.

The functions you need are simple. These are:

✓ Install one or more applications
✓ Uninstall one or more applications
✓ Select **all** applications
✓ Unselect **all** applications

It is unimaginable that any built-in application installer would not support these basic functions, but if your installer will not, you can certainly pull one from the online stores that does.

When you invoke this application, it lists *every* "APK" file resident on your android system. Note, that we did not say "resident on your android box." We said "resident on your android *system.*" That means there is a difference.

Then, you should expect to list **all** APK files on your external **hard drive**, assuming that you have one connected to your android TV system. Yes. Additionally, all APK files on your USB flash drive will load, and yes – every APK file from your SD card will list as well but, that's just what you see up front.

The directory "APK Cleanup Image" directory has a very special purpose, based on a somewhat useful peculiarity. *All of your APK files list in the order that your android system finds them in your disk directories – **sorted*** *by directory.*

Huh? What? Come again?

Ok. That **is** a bit of a head full. Let us elaborate to see if we cannot clear things up a little. The question would seem to be; does any of this cranial complication really aid us to build a more stable android TV environment? Perhaps not, but it ***does*** make system restoration much easier.

If the files list in *order*, and sort by **directory**, then the files in the "APK Cleanup Image" directory will list in order, as well. The listing order will **confine** itself to this directory, *before considering files from any other.* Thus, if you load this directory with APK files, these files will list in order when you call for the application **un**-installer.

This is a super-cool function of your AMS restore system, as it makes removing these **pre-installed** applications a **snap**. You will find all *automatically installed applications* listed **in order**, probably at the **top** of the application list, in your installer.

Remove ALL of these applications, first thing after resetting your system. Just go down the line and mark them, then order them "uninstalled" with the single press of one button.

Delete any remaining APK files

When moving your APK files to the "external media" (SD card or USB flash) you should be using the "Copy" command (not "Move" or similar) command to move your files. This will *protect* your APK files until you can **verify** the transfer. After _safely_ transferring **all** APK files to the external media, you should delete any APK files remaining on your system.

BACKUP your directories for easy restore

We have already talked about this at length. Just remember that the whole reason to back up to external memory is to have clean system rebuild tools right at your fingertips.

Power failures, memory corruption, system crashes are all meaningless to the clean APK file stores safely archived to your SD card or USB flash drive.

That said, who knows what evil *lurks* in the shadows. Your SD card or USB drive could fail, taking your clean file archives with it. This is **extremely** unlikely, but if you are the careful type, you will have a **backup** of these clean files on another medium, tucked away for safety.

Set up your remote AC clicker –

You will use this switch to "remote reboot" your android TV box. You may laugh until you have used it for the first time. **Then**, you will become a fast believer.

Plug the remote controlled *switch* into your home AC outlet and the *android box* into the remote controlled outlet on the switch.

You may consider going forward without this switch, but we *strenuously* resist that suggestion. Without a remote outlet, you will be hopping up and down like a kangaroo when rebooting your android box, whereas all that is *actually* required - is for you to press a single button.

It should be evident by now that the AMS restore system is not an application – it is a *process*. This switch is part of the AMS *process* for seizing real control over your android TV box. Do NOT omit it.

REMOVE the File Manager and Extractor –

You likely will not need to use the extractor again for a very long time – if ever. So, what do we do?

All together now…

We remove it! It has the potential to crash your system, even if you are **not** using it. Remove it now, and restore it from your safe archives when again you have real need for it.

REBOOT your android TV Box –

Your AMS restore system build is complete. **Reboot** your box to ensure that the system and memory is clean and ready for use.

In the event that you suffer a crash as a result of all this activity, never fear; your restore system is here. You may RESET your system instead, and use the restore kit to return it to functionality.

Part Five – The Proof

Let There be Light: A Practical Example...

If you have been having trouble with your android box, and you have not already done so, **reset your TV box**, and we will proceed to set it up. If it has been clean, you may simply reboot it.

Do not blink, as things will go by rather quickly. Let us begin...

➢ *(Reboot or reset your android TV system and boot to desktop.*

Now, let us consider the following...

You are watching one of your favorite streaming services when your TV box crashes! The display on your TV monitor freezes TIGHT. It will not advance.

First step: Use the "back" button to return to the desktop, if possible. From here, you can decide to **replace** the failing application (from the stores in your backup image directory), **reboot** the android box, **blow** the caches, **reset** the box, or take whatever steps you feel necessary.

Hint: In this situation, you would likely *replace the failing application.*

➢ *Use the application installer to "mark" the application, select "Uninstall." After uninstall completes (takes a second, or so) then select "Install" to replace the application. Then try your application again.*

We hope that you are now back up and running again, with no problem. This is very often the way it happens.

Then again, very often it is **not**. If the offending application will *not* install, or installation has made no difference, then you should **reboot**. Remember that YOU placed the APK files that list in the application installer. They are *certainly* clean, so the **system** *must be compromised...*

➢ **Reboot** *your android TV box.*

Use your "remote clicker" to reboot your android TV box.

Every time you press your "clicker," your android box will reboot. Usually, you will need several boots to reach a good desktop, but that's just the way things are.

How long you wait between reboots is flexible – and *could* affect your reboot results. However, you will usually get good results if you wait around 20 seconds. You will probably cut this timing down to half, with practice.

If your system will NOT reboot after three or four tries, you should consider your option to **reset** your android TV box, using the hardware reset button.

This example is very simple, and is but **one** of myriad possible scenarios. That is why you need an AMS system to manage things. Properly maintaining an android TV box is a **complex** process.

The key thing to learn from *this* example is that your android restore system does **not** work alone. It needs YOU, thinking, and willing to try different things. The AMS restore system infrastructure then seeks to make it *easy* for you to try them.

When rebooting your system, take **note** of how it behaves. Watch your system carefully as it reboots. Try to *infer* whether each boot is getting better or worse. This information will guide your next theory – and therefore your next actions.

Convergence and Divergence

As you gain experience with the reboot/reset process you will learn to determine (by system behavior) whether your system is converging *upon* a useable desktop with each reboot – or moving further *away* from it.

This is obviously an important skill to develop. It will help you to build theories that will define the *tipping point* between when you should reboot and when to reset your android box. This restore system makes the difference between reboot and reset nearly identical – but only "*nearly.*"

There remain advantages to reboot over reset. The *pre-installed* applications do **not** automatically install at *reboot*, for one thing – and therefore you need not bother to remove them. That fact alone makes reboots somewhat faster (though not much) but there are other things too that make reboot preferable.

If, after several boots you notice that the environment is moving *toward* a clean boot (convergence), you should reboot again. The next boot or two should produce a useable desktop and avoid the reset altogether. Even FIVE reboots is reasonable, if each boot moves you *noticeably* toward convergence (watch the network).

If, however your system exhibits network problems, reports a machine check (never mind what that is) reports google play errors or displays other serious anomalies, moving it *farther* from a clean system (divergence) then you should "soft-reset" your android box using the system menus. In this situation, your android system failure is beyond your ability to repair it.

Take note though, that reaching the desktop in and of itself means little. It might *look* great, but STILL be failing. For confidence, **test the network** and run the file application installer that they behave normally, and you are probably on a good desktop.

A Flash Quiz

Using the AMS requires experience and intuition. You cannot simply read this manual and decide on anything. You have to **build it out**, and begin actually to *control* your android system using this tool before you **really** see the benefits. It's like drinking coffee. You need to consume several cups over several weeks before you *really* start to "get it."

In addition to the *freedom* offered by the AMS tool itself, you will gain additional *stability* – just by **using** it. Day by day, **you** will learn what applications cause **you** trouble, and the kinds of trouble **you** can expect from them. You will theorize and approach problems with your android TV box smartly. You will devise ways to deal with specific applications so that when using them, they have a minimum effect on **your** android TV box environment.

Yes, we said it before – but this seems a good place to **repeat** it...

AMS restore system is all about YOU. AMS is NOT a magic bullet. It is a **tool**, nothing more, though it is a very **powerful** tool. Fueled by *your* imagination, the AMS restore system is able to deal with virtually any problem that might plague your android system.

Consider this scenario carefully:

There is an application on your android TV box that you like to keep handy. **You do not want to have to install it every time that boot your android system since you use it daily.**

The application works cleanly long enough for you to make practical use of it (a couple of days), so that you can use it freely. However, this application is particularly volatile **over time**. *That is, if left standing on your TV box, the system will crash.*

You do not want to remove the application, as you want to resume each new session **with this application in place** *- on a* **clean** *system.*

Q: *What to do?*

A: For *this* scenario, you might *replace* the application with a NEW version (takes seconds with this system) and *leave the new version in place* for next time you boot your TV box. This new version direct from your clean archives will **not** commence to corrupt *until the application runs.*

However, we **know** that the application will run **cleanly** for a couple of days, which is more than enough time to get us through our need of it today.

Then, before shutting down, just replace the application with a fresh one and your two days will **never** expire. This keeps the application from crashing the system when it is not in use.

Cool huh?

You see then that AMS restore system, coupled with your intuition and reason forms a very special product that you simply cannot *buy* anywhere. You cannot simply pluck this kit from the shelf. You have to roll your own, but at least you have this AMS construction guide to lead you there.

The work to put this AMS kit together is not hard, but that is irrelevant. Hard work produces uncommon results. That IS what we are seeking here: uncommon results.

What If My Box NEVER Crashes

On first thought, this might seem a curious question, but actually, it has great relevance, because even if your android box is stable and NEVER crashes, you STILL need AMS system.

The average android box gets **dirtier** every time you use it. Over time, it will grow slow and sluggish. It will exhibit strange behaviors. Eventually, you **will** need to clean the system, as the only way to optimize it.

The "cleaning" process will force you to wipe your entire android box clean.

This means formatting the system (there is no hard drive) and rebuilding it from scratch. **None** of your data will survive the process. EVERYTHING would be lost.

The solution? Simply apply this AMS restore strategy and you will be up and running again - just where you left off - in minutes! That is about as "ready" as anybody needs to be.

About The Author

Mason Bolton was born and raised in San Francisco, California. He is a retired engineer, who has worked professionally in many engineering disciplines including electronics design, computer CPU design, and computer networking design. Obviously he has degrees, but why bore your with them. He is married with children and grandchildren, and has always had a passion for all things video. After retiring, he decided to "cut the cable" and his search for great alternative content led him to the android TV box. After some testing and experimentation, he devised **Android Management System**, for those seeking to make better use of the marvelous android TV environment. *"How to Build a Stable Management System for Android TV Boxes,"* was written for **you**.

Have fun!

References

The AMS Prime Directives:

- You must **ALWAYS** CHECK YOUR NETWORK WHENEVER YOU REBOOT/RESET your android TV box, even after a simple power-down.

- Be **quick** to reset your android TV box, any time you determine that your **network** application does not function properly.

- Reboot your box **several times**, until you get a stable boot.

- Reset your TV box only *once*. A second reset is rarely necessary.

- *Keep Your Android TV Box CLEAN! This is rule number one. Install only what you need to use at the moment and remove stuff you won't use for a time.*

- *Android TV box memory is easily corrupted. It is just so vital to keep this in mind when you are debugging a crash.*

- *ALWAYS raise your network via the blue button on your access point!*

- *ALWAYS use the built-in applications where possible.*

- *Avoid corrupted applications: MOVE TO EXTERNAL MEDIA.*

- *NEVER log onto any application including email and google play services.*

- *You may FREELY log onto any application (email, twitter, an online account) IF you do so online using the built-in browser. Do NOT use* **applications** *requiring you to log on.*

NEVER log on to Google Play Services. If you do so, it will update your environment with untested (from the perspective of your TV box) updates and *applications. An android phone might **love** these updates, but they can **blow** your android TV system apart.*

- Determine the "quiescent state" of your android TV box.

- REMOVE any volatile apps before leaving your system standing for a time.

Stable Program Reference

- Adobe Acrobat 18.2.0.182935.apk

Yep, our old friend. Permits reading and working with APK files.

- Advanced Task Manager 6.4.0.apk

A fun program to kill tasks, free up memory, save battery life, and more...

- Alarm-clock-2-7-1.apk

Everybody needs an alarm clock. Set this one from your easy chair!

- APK Export 3.2.4.apk

Your APK extractor. Like a parachute, you will not need it often, but when you need it, you'll really need it.

- File Manager 1.12.17.apk

Goes beyond the file browser for directory creation, file management and more...

- Finance 3.2.2.apk

Yahoo finance. Keep up with your investments right from your easy chair.

- Ghostery-privacy-browser-2-0-7.apk

Next best thing to a VPN for keeping your surfing activities private.

- Jota-text-editor-0-2-35-multi-android.apk

A text editor is a vital tool for any fully capable computer system.

- LastPass Password Manager Premium 4.4.1842.apk

Use one logon to store ALL your passwords for easy login. It works well, but you STILL should not log onto your android system. Make any logons online.

- Pdf-reader-3-2-4.apk

This PDF reader has proven itself to be very stable.

- Pdf-reader-5-9.apk

Another GREAT application for reading PDF files.

- Rotation Control 1.0.apk*

Need to rotate your screen orientation for a particular application. Try this tool...

- VLC 3.0.11.apk*

A full-featured video streamers. Offered for completeness. You should use only default streamers with your restore kit.

- WiFi Automatic 1.7.8.apk

Might offer relief with some unstable networks.

- WiFiReEnabler 1.10.20130722.apk

Might help stabilize network dropping.

- YouTube 13.24.59.apk* -- DO NOT USE

www.ingramcontent.com/pod-product-compliance
Lightning Source LLC
Chambersburg PA
CBHW020329290526
45785CB00007B/2980